Eat Your Way To

TRUE

Love

LAGOON BOOKS

Project Editor: Sylvia Goulding
Book Design: Norma Martin

Thanks to Mike Goulding, Lesley Robb, Simon Farnhell, Ray Leaning, Nick Daws and Ann Marangos
Cover Design: River Design. www.riverdesign.com

Series Editor: Lucy Dear
Visual concept: Sarah Wells
Based on original concept by Simon Melhuish

Published by:
LAGOON BOOKS
PO BOX 311, KT2 5QW, UK
PO BOX 990676, Boston, MA 02199, USA
www.lagoongames.com

ISBN: 1902813626

Printed in Hong Kong.

Eat Your Way To **TRUE** Love

Introduction

Ever felt that love has passed you by? Most likely it's not you, it's your cooking. Food is the fuel for romance—and, sadly, if you can't deliver the goods, chances are you'll find yourself stranded on the hard shoulder of love, waiting for Emergency Rescue to mend your broken heart. But now there's no more need to suffer: This book will show you the road to your private Shangri-la...

Let's Party

In the fun-packed first chapter of this book you'll find a selection of recipes to grace any celebration, from summer barbecue to midwinter ball. Whether you're partying *à deux* or in a huge crowd with all your friends—delicious party food from *Spinach and Cheese Tartlets* to *Tuck-in Turkey Tacos* will set the scene. Romance is sure to be in the air.

Dinin' by Candlelight

Draw the curtains... dim the lights... and get set for some serious romancing. We've trawled the world for deliciously intimate dishes, ranging from *Fragrant Lamb Pilau* to *Velvety Venus Casserole*, from *Angels on Horseback* to *Soulful Sole in Port*. There's no doubt about it—two will soon become one when you share these romantic recipes steeped in love.

Sweet Sensations

On to desserts, and a host of delectable dishes in Chapter 3 will round off your meal to perfection. Will you tempt your sweetie with *Hot-and-Cold Love Cups*, or take them to a South Sea paradise with *Tropical Fruit Fondue*? Whatever you choose, chances are the sweet sensations won't end when you leave the table...

Sealed with a Kiss

Finally, all lovers know it's better to give than to receive, and the edible gifts in Chapter 4 will assure your place in your lover's affections. From *Romantic Rum Truffles* to *Melt-in-the-Mouth Cherries*, these delightful confections will demonstrate your undying love beyond doubt. But be sure you keep one or two for yourself as well...

And there you have it—your amazing secret recipe for romance! With a little help from these delightful dishes, the path to true love really can run smooth for you. No longer will you have to stand alone and watch as your friends go down the aisle two by two. Romance is within your grasp, so why wait any longer? Turn over the page now and start cooking. Your true love is hungry...

Chapter 1

Let's Party!

Love is in the Air—Bring a Taste of
Passion to your Celebrations...

It's your party—
and you can eat
what you want
to...

Contents

Late-Nite Energy Sandwich

These red-blooded sandwiches will keep you dancing till dawn.

Serves 8

What to buy

- 900 g/2 lb rump steak
- 8 small or 4 large ciabattas or other bread, cut in half
- 4 tbsp olive oil
- 2 tbsp French mustard
- 2 tbsp lemon juice
- Salt and pepper
- A handful of fresh rosemary and thyme, chopped
- 8 handfuls of mixed salad leaves

How to cook it...

⭐ Lay the meat on the work surface and flatten with a wooden spoon. Cut into eight equal portions.

⭐ In a small bowl, combine the oil, mustard, lemon juice, and salt and pepper to taste. Place the steaks in a large shallow bowl and cover with the marinade. Cover and chill for 30 minutes.

⭐ Remove the steaks from the bowl and flash-fry in a large, hot frying pan. Cut the ciabattas open, fill with the steaks, and pour over the juices from the pan. Top with salad, and the other bread half.

⭐ Serve—and watch them disappear faster than you can say "bon appetit."

He who eats alone,
chokes alone...
(Arab Proverb)

Pick a Stick

The chicken in this dish will taste fantastic if threaded
onto a kebab (kabob) stick and grilled over an open
barbecue fire at a hot summer party. The kebab (kabob)
will work its magic and bewitch your favorite guy or gal—
it's just like a culinary version of Cupid's arrow!

Greek Love-God Chicken

Bring out the Love God in your special guest with this legendary Greek recipe.

Serves 4

What to buy

- 1 tbsp fresh mint, chopped
- 1 tbsp fresh coriander (cilantro), chopped
- 1 tsp ground coriander
- 1 tsp ground cumin
- A pinch of salt
- Juice of 2 limes
- 4 chicken breasts, skinned and cut into strips
- 150 g/5 oz Greek-style yogurt
- 150 g/5 oz hummus
- 2 tbsp olive oil
- 4 Greek breads (pitta bread)
- Mixed salad leaves, shredded

How to cook it...

⭐ In a bowl blend together the herbs, spices, and lime juice. Put the chicken strips into the marinade and turn to coat evenly. Chill for 1 hour.

⭐ Combine the yogurt and the hummus, cover with clingfilm (plastic wrap) and chill.

⭐ Heat the oil in a large frying pan. Stir-fry the chicken for 5-10 minutes, until golden.

⭐ Warm and halve the Greek breads. Fill each pocket with chicken strips, yogurt-hummus mixture and salad leaves.

⭐ Put on a smooth dance record, then serve— watch everyone else dive to the food while you dance with your heartthrob.

Marinade, then Serenade

A marinade is a great way of tenderizing meat and imparting flavor to it. It must contain oil and something acidic (vinegar or lemon juice), but you can choose your own spices—the chicken will cook quickly and taste divine—just like his kisses!

If music be the food of love, play on... (William Shakespeare)

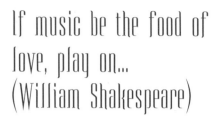

Spice it up

FOR A GUARANTEED LOVE EXPERIENCE, SERVE THE SUMMER LOVIN' CHICKEN WITH A SPICY SALSA DIP AND THE SPARKLY SPRITZY LEMONADE FROM THIS BOOK. WATCH THE MOOD HOT UP, AS PALATES BECOME INFLAMED AND CHEEKS FLUSHED FROM THE BUBBLY ALCOHOLIC DRINK! NOW MAKE YOUR MOVE!

Let's Party!

Summer-Lovin' Chicken

These sizzling chickens are perfect party fare—whether you're soaking up the summer sun or dancing under the stars with your one true love.

Serves 4

What to buy

- 2 baby chickens, spatchcocked
- 125 ml/4 fl oz/½ cup olive oil
- 6 tbsp lemon juice
- 2 tbsp mixed peppercorns, crushed coarsely
- Sea salt
- Lemon wedges, to serve

How to cook it...

⭐ Put the baby chickens in a dish and make several slashes across them with a sharp knife.

⭐ Combine the oil, lemon juice, and peppercorns, and brush the chickens with the mixture, working it into the cuts. Cover and leave to marinate for at least 4 hours.

⭐ Prepare the barbecue. Season the skin side of the chickens, then place them skin side down on the barbecue. Cook for 15 minutes, then turn over and cook for a further 10 minutes.

⭐ Remove the chickens from the grill and cut each bird in half lengthwise. Serve with lemon wedges, ice-cold beer, and sizzling hot summer party music.

Food is not about impressing people. It's about making them feel comfortable...
(Ina Garten)

Healthy Peas

Chickpeas are high in soluble fiber, which is great for digestion and reduces cholesterol. Chickpeas and other legumes are a main component of the Mediterranean diet. Nutritionists and doctors worldwide have recently discovered its fantastic health benefits—share its great tastes and pleasures with your beloved.

Eastern Spice

A PAKORA IS AN INDIAN VEGETABLE PATTIE, SIMILAR TO A BHAJI. THEY MAKE FOR IDEAL PARTY FINGER FOOD, AND ARE GREAT FOR DIPPING INTO ALL SORTS OF SPICY ACCOMPANIMENTS.

Eastern-Promise Pakoras

Add a little spice to the night—with the promise of more to come—with these beguiling tempters.

Makes 25

What to buy

- 200 g/7 oz chick-pea flour
- 2 tsp curry powder
- 1 tsp salt
- 2 carrots, finely diced
- 2 large potatoes, finely diced
- 2 onions, finely diced
- 3 tbsp fresh parsley, chopped
- Vegetable oil for deep-frying
- Chutney and yogurt to serve

How to cook it...

⭐ Make a batter from the flour, spices, salt, and 150 ml/5 fl oz water. Cover and leave to rest.

⭐ Stir the carrot, potato, onion, and parsley into the batter.

⭐ In a large pan, heat the oil. Add the batter, one tablespoon at a time, and fry until brown. Lift out with a slotted spoon and leave the pakoras to drain on kitchen paper.

⭐ Serve with plain yogurt and a selection of chutneys, and feed one to your favorite person with the promise of things to come.

Spinach and Cheese Tartlets

It gave Popeye strength – just think what the spinach in this recipe can do for your love life!

Makes 16

What to buy

- 125 g/4 ½ oz flour
- Salt and pepper
- 60 g/2 ½ oz cold butter
- Butter for greasing the molds
- 1 tbsp olive oil
- 2 small shallots, chopped
- 1 garlic clove, crushed
- 125 g/4 ½ oz leaf spinach, finely chopped
- 100 g/4 oz goats' cheese, diced
- 1 large egg
- 125 ml/4 fl oz milk

How to cook it...

In a large bowl, combine the flour, salt, butter, and 2–3 tbsp cold water, and knead together until you have a smooth dough. Cover with clingfilm (plastic wrap) and chill for about 1 hour.

Heat the oven to 200°C/400°F/Gas Mark 6. Shape the dough into 16 even-sized balls. Roll out each ball to a circle. Grease 16 greased molds (about 60 ml/2 fl oz each), then line them with the pastry circles.

Heat the oil and fry the shallots for about 5 minutes, or until they are lightly brown; add the garlic and the spinach. Cover and leave to cook on a low heat for 3–4 minutes.

⭐ Stir the cheese into the spinach mixture. In a bowl, whisk together the egg and the milk. Stir into the spinach mixture. Pour mixture into the molds and bake for 25 minutes.

⭐ Leave to cool, then serve for a tasty snack break, before the action heats up again.

There's no greater love than the love of food...
(George Bernard Shaw)

Carry on Partying

Spinach is one of the those great vegetables that will let you party into a ripe old age. A good source of immune-boosting beta carotene, calcium and iron, it will strengthen your bones and prevent anaemia. It is also likely to protect against the age-related eye disease AMD. Don't stop, party on!

Tuck-in Turkey Tacos

Magic! Put out a bowl of these toothsome tacos at your party, and watch them disappear before your eyes.

Serves 4

What to buy

- 2 tbsp vegetable oil
- 450 g/1 lb minced turkey
- 1 large onion, chopped
- 2 garlic cloves, crushed
- 3 red chilies, chopped
- 1 tsp chili powder
- 1 tbsp paprika
- 1 tsp ground cumin
- 2 tbsp tomato purée
- 425 g/15 oz can red kidney beans
- 400 g/14 oz can chopped tomatoes
- 2 red (bell) peppers, cut into strips
- 8 taco shells

How to cook it...

Heat the oven to 170°C/325°F/Gas Mark 3. In a large ovenproof pan, heat the oil. Add the turkey, onion, garlic, and chilies, and fry for about 5 minutes, or until the meat is browned and the onion softened. Add the spices and tomato purée.

Drain and rinse the kidney beans, then add them to the pan together with the tomatoes, and bring to the boil. Cover and cook in the oven for about 1-2 hours, stirring occasionally. After 1 hour, add the (bell) peppers.

Take the casserole out of the oven, leaving it switched on, and check the seasoning. If the chili is very liquid, place it on top of the stove and boil rapidly, with the lid off, to reduce a little. Meanwhile warm the taco shells in the oven.

✪ Place the casserole on a heatproof surface, the taco shells on a large plate, and put out bowls of soured cream, guacamole, and grated cheese. Now let the party start in earnest—everyone help themselves and have a real good time.

She'll make you take your clothes off/And go dancing in the rain/She'll make you live her crazy life/But she'll take away your pain/Like a bullet to your brain...(Livin' la Vida Loca)

Pile on the Fun

Sour cream, guacamole, chopped chilies, and tomato are great in tacos. Follow with Iced Mexicans, and the party will be in full swing.

Your words are my food, your breath my wine. You are everything to me... (Sarah Bernhardt)

Much-loved Pizzas

Pizzas were first served in New York in 1905, at Lombardi's. Since then they have become the world's favorite food, with toppings ranging from Thai to Mexican, and even including baked beans!

Dance all Nite

THE SIRTAKI—AS DANCED IN THE FILM "ZORBA THE GREEK"—IS AN ALL-TIME PARTY FAVORITE, PROVIDED YOU'VE DRUNK ENOUGH AND HAVE LOST YOUR INHIBITIONS. IT'S ALSO A GREAT EXCUSE TO PUT YOUR ARM AROUND YOUR LOVED ONE AND STUMBLE AROUND INTOXICATED BY LOVE...

Let's Party!

Greek Pizza

This Greek version of the Italian favourite is made for partying—even if the party is just you and your sweetie!

Serves 8

What to buy

- 4 pizza bases, about 22 cm/9 in diameter
- 2 garlic cloves, crushed
- 6 tbsp olive oil
- 8 tbsp tomato purée
- 8 beefsteak tomatoes, sliced
- 2 aubergines (eggplants), sliced
- 2 red (bell) peppers, cut into strips
- 2 yellow (bell) peppers, cut into strips
- 250 g/8 oz goats' cheese, crumbled
- 1 tbsp fresh oregano, chopped
- 1 tbsp fresh thyme, chopped

How to cook it...

⬠ Heat the oven according to the pizza base instruction. Place bases on a baking sheet. Mix together the garlic and 4 tbsp of the oil, then lightly brush bases with the mixture. Evenly cover with the tomato purée.

⬠ Arrange tomato and aubergine (eggplant) slices and (bell) pepper strips on the pizza bases. Crumble over the goats' cheese and sprinkle with chopped herbs. Drizzle the remaining oil over the top.

⬠ Bake the pizzas on the top shelf of the oven for about 10-15 minutes.

⬠ Cut into wedges and serve immediately, while playing a Greek Sirtaki on the hifi.

World Party

Skewered meat is global: the Portuguese call it 'espetadas', in the Far East you find 'satay', usually served with a dipping sauce, Japan has skewered fowl called 'yakitori', in France, 'brochettes' are served, meaning skewer, and in the US we have 'kabobs'.

Chinese Fruit

KUMQUATS ARE SMALL OVAL CITRUS FRUIT, LOOKING A BIT LIKE MINIATURE ORANGES. THEY ARE EATEN WHOLE, WITH THEIR SKIN. THEIR SLIGHTLY BITTER FLAVOR MAKES THEM AN ACQUIRED TASTE, BUT THEY TASTE GREAT WHEN COOKED, AS ON THESE SKEWERS. YOUR BABY WILL BE IMPRESSED!

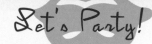

Love-at-First-Sight Lamb

One taste of this heavenly dish and your baby will be smitten for life. It's love at first bite for sure!

Serves 2

What to buy

- 1 tsp paprika
- 6 tbsp vegetable oil
- 700 g/1 ½ lb lamb, cut into small cubes
- 16 whole kumquats
- 1 green (bell) pepper, seeded and cut into chunks
- 1 red (bell) pepper, seeded and cut into chunks
- 6 tomatoes

How to cook it...

⭐ Stir the paprika into 4 tbsp of the oil, then brush the lamb with the mixture.

⭐ Thread the meat cubes onto skewers, alternating with kumquats, and green and red (bell) pepper chunks.

⭐ Place the skewers on the barbecue, brush with the remaining oil and cook for 15–20 minutes, or until cooked through.

⭐ Serve with a salad of cooked rice, sweet corn, tomato wedges, and sweet, hot kisses.

A man loses his sense of
direction after four drinks;
A woman loses hers
after four kisses...
(H.L. Mencken)

Love and Lemonade

This drink is great for a good party atmosphere—
and of course for flirting! But beware: as the
English writer Norman Douglas once wrote, "Wine
is a precarious aphrodisiac, and its fumes have
blighted many a mating." Be warned!

Eat, Drink ...

THIS RECIPE ORIGINATES FROM
GERMANY, WHERE IT IS KNOWN
AS 'COLD DUCK'. ITS STRANGE
NAME IS BASED ON THE
SPECIAL DUCK-SHAPED JUG
FOR MAKING THE DRINK: AN
INSET TUBE IS FILLED WITH
ICE CUBES, THUS MAKING SURE
THE DRINK IS NOT DILUTED—
FOR MAXIMUM IMPACT!

Sparkly Spritzy Lemonade

Your party is sure to sparkle with this grown-up lemonade—make sure you save some for yourself!

Serves 8–10

What to buy

- 2 untreated lemons
- 1 tbsp caster (superfine) sugar
- 2 bottles of white wine
- 2 bottles of Champagne or sparkling wine
- A shot of orange liqueur (optional)
- Ice cubes

How to cook it...

⭐ Thinly slice the lemons and place in a large pitcher. Sprinkle the sugar over the lemons, then top with the two bottles of wine.

⭐ Leave in a cool place for at least 12 hours for the flavors to mingle.

⭐ When you are ready to party, add plenty of ice cubes, crack open the Champagne and add to the drink. If you want to add extra "kick" just add a shot of orange liqueur.

⭐ Enjoy—and remember it's not really lemonade!

Great Variations

THIS RECIPE IS ENDLESSLY VARIABLE—TRY VODKA, RUM, OR BRANDY INSTEAD OF THE TEQUILA, AND USE A VARIETY OF DIFFERENT FLAVORED ICE CREAMS. WATER ICES, OR SORBETS, ARE BEST. TRY ORANGE, LEMON, AND LIME.

Always do sober what you said you'd do drunk. That will teach you to keep your mouth shut... (Ernest Hemingway)

The Early Bird

Tequila does not always necessarily have a worm in it; the worm is merely a marketing tool. However, it's always got great party potential...

Iced Mexicans

Chill out with these wickedly cool cocktails—the perfect pick-up for parched partygoers!

Serves 24

What to buy

- 300 ml/10 fl oz tequila
- 4 x 600 ml/35 fl oz tubs lemon ice
- A large plateful of lime wedges
- A bucket of ice cubes

How to cook it...

⭐ Put the tequila into the freezer the day before the party—it won't freeze unless you have bought an inferior low-alcohol brand!

⭐ Just before the party, fill a large shallow bowl (or the bathtub!) with ice cubes and park your tequila glasses in among the ice.

⭐ When you're ready to serve the Mexicans, scoop out a ball of lemon ice for each glass, pour a shot of tequila over it and serve straightaway. A refreshingly cool interlude for flushed lovers.

Chapter 2

Dinin' by Candlelight

Alone at last—Food to Share for Romantic Nights...

Serve a tasty
meal for a tender
evening...

Contents

Silky Smooth Soup

Banish the cares of the day with this velvety soup. Soon your sweetie will have eyes only for you...

Serves 2

What to buy

- 1 large ripe avocado
- 2 tsp lemon juice
- 200 ml/7 fl oz fresh chicken stock
- 2 tsp dry sherry
- 1 tbsp single (light) cream
- Salt and pepper
- 1 tbsp fresh chives, snipped

How to cook it...

⭐ Peel and halve the avocado, discard the stone. In a bowl, purée the avocado flesh together with the lemon juice.

⭐ Gradually stir in the stock, sherry, and cream. Stir to blend thoroughly. Season to taste, and chill for at least 1 hour.

⭐ Sprinkle the chives over the chilled soup, and serve with thin slices of toast. Pour a glass of chilled white wine or dry white sherry.

Why, then the world's mine oyster, which I with sword will open...
(William Shakespeare)

High-Octane Food

OYSTERS ARE LOW IN FAT AND RICH IN MANY MINERALS, SUCH AS PHOSPHORUS, AND IODINE. THEY ARE ALSO ONE OF THE RICHEST SOURCES OF ZINC, AND IT IS THIS MINERAL WHICH HAS LED TO SOME OF THE LOVE-LIFE ENHANCING CLAIMS MADE OF OYSTERS. THERE MAY, IN FACT, BE A PEARL OF TRUTH IN IT. WHY NOT FIND OUT FOR YOURSELF?

Oysters and Love

Already in Roman times, oysters had a raunchy reputation, and Casanova certainly believed in their amorous effect: he is said to have eaten 50 of them every morning in the bath, together with his favorite lady of the moment!

Dinin' by Candlelight

"Angels on Horseback"

It's true—oysters are the food of love. Serve these to your beloved and watch them melt in your hand...

Makes 8

What to buy

- 🐚 8 oysters
- 🐚 A pinch of Cayenne pepper
- 🐚 1 tbsp lemon juice
- 🐚 4 rashers (strips) of bacon, cut in half
- 🐚 8 small slices of bread
- 🐚 A handful of rocket leaves

How to cook it...

⭐ Heat the oven to 200°C/400°F/Gas Mark 6. Sprinkle the oysters with Cayenne pepper and lemon juice. Wrap each one in a half slice of bacon and fasten with a cocktail stick.

⭐ Place an oyster and bacon roll on each slice of bread. Bake in the oven for about 15 minutes until both the oyster and the bacon are cooked.

⭐ Serve the angels on a bed of rocket, feed them to your lover, and watch him fall deeper and deeper in love with you.

Fish, to taste right,
must swim three times—
in water, in butter,
and in wine...
(Polish Proverb)

Fish Families

THE SOLE IS A FLAT FISH—
LIKE THE HALIBUT AND THE
PLAICE—ALL OF WHICH ARE
ALSO WHITE FISH. ALTHOUGH
NOT AS NUTRITIOUS AS THE
OILY FISH, WHITE FISH HAVE A
MORE DELICATE FLAVOR, AND
ARE LOWER IN CALORIES,
LEAVING YOU AS SLIM AND
ADORABLE AS WHEN YOU
FIRST MET EACH OTHER!

Fated to be Mated

The Zodiac sign of Pisces is a double sign of fish—
the male principle plus the female principle—representing
the fecundity of the fish and their rapid procreation.
The fish, when eaten, passes on its fertility, and it is also
said to bring prosperity to the diner.

Dinin' by Candlelight

Soulful Sole in Port

Raise the temperature with these fragrant fish. You'll be the 'sole' object of your darling's desires.

Serves 2

What to buy

- 4 small sole fillets (about 75 g/3oz each)
- Juice of ½ lemon
- Salt and pepper
- 3 tbsp plain (all-purpose) flour
- 2 tbsp olive oil
- 125 g/4 ½ oz mushrooms, thinly sliced
- 1 garlic clove, crushed
- 4 spring onions (scallions), sliced into rings
- 125 ml/4 fl oz white port or sherry

How to cook it...

Place the sole fillets next to each other on a platter and drizzle with half the lemon juice. Season with salt and pepper, then chill in the fridge.

Turn the fish fillets in flour. Heat 1 tbsp oil in a frying pan and fry the fish until golden brown. Remove and keep warm in a low oven.

Put the remaining oil in the pan and fry the mushrooms for 3 minutes. Add the garlic and the onions, cook over a gentle heat for 2 minutes. Season to taste, then add the port. Bring to the boil and cook for a further 3 minutes.

Light the candles, turn the lights down low and serve, with a glass of dry white port.

Surprise Potato Cakes

Everyone loves a surprise, especially when it's a bit spicy.
Titillate your sweetie with these moreish morsels.

Serves 2

What to buy

- 🦞 200 g/7 oz potatoes
- 🦞 200 g/7 oz sweet potatoes
- 🦞 1 tbsp Thai curry paste
- 🦞 1 tbsp chopped fresh coriander (cilantro)
- 🦞 1 tbsp plain (all-purpose) flour, for dusting
- 🦞 2 tbsp vegetable oil
- 🦞 Lime wedges to serve

Surprisingly fiery salsa

- 🦞 100 g/4 oz tomatoes, chopped
- 🦞 ½ red onion, chopped
- 🦞 1 large red chili, chopped
- 🦞 1 cm/½ in piece root ginger, grated
- 🦞 1 garlic clove, chopped
- 🦞 3 tbsp white wine vinegar
- 🦞 25 g/1 oz sugar

How to cook it...

🦞 Cook all the potatoes for 15 minutes until softened, then drain. Mash the potatoes and then mix together with the curry paste and coriander (cilantro). With lightly floured hands, shape into 8 cakes. Dust with flour.

🦞 Heat the oil in a frying pan, and fry cakes in batches for about 3–4 minutes, turning once.

Make the surprisingly fiery salsa. Put all the ingredients into a large pan. Bring to the boil, and simmer for 5 minutes until thickened. Serve with the potato cakes and lime wedges.

 Watch your lover's eyes light up with gastronomic delight as you serve your sweet potato cakes.

 Sharing food with another human being is an intimate act that should not be indulged in lightly...
(M.F.K. Fisher)

Sweet Nothings

Despite its name, the sweet potato is not, in fact, related to the potato, but you can treat it in much the same way. Boiled, mashed, baked, or roasted, its slightly sweet taste will make a change from the ordinary potato, and be a surprise for your darling's tastebuds!

Spice-up-your-Lovelife Pasta

Get cosy with this delicious dish. The creamy sauce and spicy sausage go together so well...

Serves 2

What to buy

- 4 tsp sunflower oil
- 1 red onion, finely sliced
- 2 tsp sugar
- 200 g/7 oz chorizo sausage, skinned and cut into bite-size pieces (or other sausage)
- 2 red onions, roughly chopped
- 2 garlic cloves, crushed
- 400 g/14 oz cherry tomatoes
- 2 tbsp tomato purée
- 1 tbsp chili sauce
- Salt and pepper
- 350 g/12 oz pasta twists

How to cook it...

⚝ Heat half the oil in a frying pan. Add the onion slices and 1 tsp sugar, and cook over a high heat for 8-10 minutes, until crispy. Lift out and drain on kitchen paper.

⚝ In a large frying pan, dry-fry the chorizo for 2-3 minutes, until the oil starts to run out. Add the remaining sunflower oil and fry the onion and garlic for 3-4 minutes, until soft.

⚝ Add the tomatoes, tomato purée, chili sauce, and the remaining sugar, and season to taste. Simmer for about 10 minutes, or until the sauce has thickened a little.

⚝ Meanwhile cook the pasta and drain. Return to the pan and add the sauce. Serve in bowls topped with crispy onion, accompanied by a full-bodied red wine such as a Cabernet Sauvignon or a Merlot, to share with your full-blooded lover.

Life is a combination of magic and pasta... (Federico Fellini)

Spice is Nice

This dish combines chili sauce and chorizo, a Spanish paprika-flavored sausage. It will leave you flushed, as if you'd just fallen in love!

Velvety Venus Casserole

This heartwarming dish from Portugal is perfect for turning up the heat on a cold winter's night.

Serves 2

What to buy

- 4 tbsp olive oil
- 1 onion, roughly chopped
- 2 garlic cloves, chopped
- 1 green (bell) pepper, cut into strips
- 60 ml/2 fl oz beef stock
- 60 ml/2 fl oz dry white wine
- 200 g/7 oz pork fillet
- 200 g/7 oz tomatoes, skinned and sliced
- Salt and pepper
- 2 handfuls of fresh coriander (cilantro) and parsley, chopped
- 100 g/4 oz clams
- Long-grained rice, to serve

How to cook it...

Put the oil into a large saucepan or casserole dish with a lid. Add onion and garlic, and cook gently, stirring occasionally, until softened. Add the (bell) pepper and cook for about 5 minutes. Add the stock and the wine and stir.

Cut the pork fillets into bite-sized pieces. Add to the pan and cook for ½ hour.

Cover the pork with the sliced tomatoes, do not stir. Season to taste and add the herbs.

Place the clams on top of the tomatoes, in their shells. Do not stir. Cover the pan, and bring to the boil. As soon as the steam starts to escape, reduce the heat and leave to simmer on a very low heat for another 15 minutes.

✡ Meanwhile, cook the rice. Serve the Venus Casserole in the dish in which it was cooked, and pass a loving spoonful to your honey-pie.

A meal without wine is like a day without sunshine... (A. Brillat-Savarin)

All at Sea

In the famous painting by Botticelli, Venus, the Roman goddess of love, rises from the sea in a clam. Is this the reason, we wonder, why clams and other shellfish have always been associated with love?

Fragrant Lamb Pilau

Spice up the night with this fragrant dish from India, then taste the spices again on your lover's lips.

Serves 2

What to buy

- 2 ½ tbsp oil
- 250 g/9 oz lamb (leg or shoulder), diced
- 1 large onion, chopped
- ¼ tsp ground coriander (cilantro)
- ¼ tsp ground cumin
- Salt and pepper
- 1 large tomato, skinned and cut into chunks
- 125 g/4 ½ oz basmati rice
- 2 cloves
- 2 cardamoms
- 2 cinnamon sticks.
- 1 tbsp chopped almonds
- 2 tbsp raisins

How to cook it...

Heat 1 tbsp oil in a large saucepan. Add the meat and half the onion, and fry for 5-10 minutes, stirring. Add the coriander (cilantro) and cumin, season to taste, then add the tomato. Heat the oven to 180°C/350°F/Gas Mark 4.

In a separate, large saucepan, heat a further 1 tbsp oil and fry the remaining onion in it. Add the rice and fry, stirring, for a few minutes. Add about 300 ml/½ pint water, the cloves, cardamoms, and cinnamon sticks. Stir to combine well, and season to taste.

Add the meat mixture to the pan with the rice. Stir to mix, cover and cook in the oven for about 45 minutes.

Heat the remaining 1/2 tbsp oil in a clean frying pan, add the almonds and raisins, and fry for about 2 minutes. Sprinkle over the pilau and serve. Your true love will definitely go for seconds.

Don't let love interfere with your appetite. It never does with mine...
(Anthony Trollope)

Pilau Please

A pilau, also known as pilaf or pilaw, is a meal-in-one. Rice, stock, meat, vegetables, herbs, and sometimes fruit are cooked together in the oven until the liquid is absorbed. It's great for lovers; get it ready in advance, and spend the time kissing not cooking!

Cast-a-Spell Country Pie

Bewitch your lover with this magic meat pie—mixed game is in the dish, and also what will follow!

Serves 4

What to buy

- 150 g/5 oz plain (all-purpose) flour
- 75 g/2 ½ oz butter, cold
- A pinch of salt
- 1 small egg and 1 egg yolk
- 450 g/1 lb, mixed game (e.g. rabbit, venison, pigeon, pheasant), chopped into bite-sized pieces
- 1 ½ tsp juniper berries
- 1 ½ tsp coarse sea salt
- 1 ½ tsp black peppercorns
- 300 ml/10 fl oz chicken stock
- 1 tbsp brandy
- ½ packet gelatin

How to cook it...

✸ Make the pastry: mix together flour, butter, and salt until the mixture resembles breadcrumbs. Beat the egg yolk with 3 tbsp cold water; mix into the pastry until the mixture forms a ball. Wrap in clingfilm (plastic wrap) and chill for 3 hours.

✸ Heat the oven to 180°C/350°F/Gas Mark 4. Roll out the pastry. Grease a loose-bottomed 18 cm/7 in cake tin. Line with a third of the pastry.

✸ Coarsely mill the juniper berries, salt, and peppercorns. Put the meat into the pastry case; season generously. Combine 1 tbsp of the stock with the brandy and add to the meat.

✸ Roll out the remaining pastry to make a cover. Cut a small circle in the center to allow steam to escape. Brush with the beaten egg. Place the pie on a baking sheet and bake in the oven for 1 hour, or until well browned.

🏵 Heat the stock, and dissolve the gelatin, set aside to cool slightly. When the pie is cooked, lift off the lid and gradually pour in the liquid.

🏵 When the pie is filled, return the lid and allow to cool for 24 hours. Serve to your love-hungry honeybun—and two hearts will beat as one.

Men always want to be a woman's first love—women like to be a man's last romance... (Oscar Wilde)

Hunting Spirit

Game is lean meat, and low in calories. Game animals (rabbits, venison, wild boar etc) are also packed with minerals such as phosphorus, magnesium, and potassium, which is why they have a reputation as a particularly stimulating, 'virile' form of food. Good hunting!

Pleasingly Tender Chicken Breasts

Romance your sweetheart with these melt-in-the-mouth chicken breasts. Another Italian masterpiece!

Serves 2

What to buy

- 2 large chicken breasts, skinned and boned
- 2 slices Cheddar cheese
- 2 slices ham
- 1 tbsp flour
- Salt and pepper
- 1 egg
- 50 g/2 oz fresh breadcrumbs
- Vegetable oil for deep-frying

How to cook it...

① Cut a pocket into each chicken breast. Push a slice of ham and a slice of cheese into each pocket.

② Spread out the flour on one plate; season generously with salt and pepper. On a second plate, crack the egg and beat it with a fork. Place the breadcrumbs on a third plate.

③ Dip the chicken first in the seasoned flour, then in the beaten egg, and finally in the breadcrumbs. Make sure the chicken is evenly coated all over, and that the breadcrumbs stick well.

Heat the oil in the deep-fryer to 190°/375°F, and deep-fry the chicken breasts for about 10-12 minutes, or until cooked through. Remove with a slotted spoon and drain on kitchen paper.

Serve with n crisp salad full of crunchy flavors and natural goodness.

Love is like a violin. The music may stop now and then, but the strings remain forever... (Unknown)

That's the Stuffing!

A typically Italian recipe, tender chicken breast stuffed with oozing cheese and succulent ham has become popular around the world. The combination of flavors and textures is exquisite, and is bound to go down a treat with your love.

Romantic Duck Salad

This light, elegant dish is no relation to Donald! It's perfect when all you want to do is gaze lovingly into each other's eyes.

Serves 2

What to buy

- 2 tbsp olive oil
- 2 tbsp fresh orange juice
- 1 garlic clove, crushed
- 1 ½ tsp ground coriander (cilantro)
- A pinch of ground mace
- A pinch of ground ginger
- Salt and pepper
- 2 duck breast fillets, about 125 g/4 oz each, skinned
- Red wine vinegar
- French mustard
- 1 tbsp clear honey
- Mixed salad leaves
- About 10 pitted black olives

How to cook it...

Heat the oven to 200°C/400°F/Gas Mark 6. In a bowl, combine 1 tbsp each of the oil and orange juice, the garlic, spices, and seasoning.

Place the duck breasts in a shallow ovenproof dish and cover with the marinade. Turn to make sure both sides are well coated. Roast in the oven for 15-20 minutes until the meat is tender.

Arrange the salad leaves on two plates. Take the duck breasts out of the dish, slice and place them on top of the salad. Distribute the olives on top. Make a dressing: whisk together the pan juices, vinegar, mustard, and honey with the remaining orange juice and oil. Season to taste and drizzle over the salad. Enjoy your lovingly prepared meal—there's plenty of time for flirting before you start and even more time for kissing once you're finished.

Cooking is like love.
It should be entered
into with abandon or
not at all...
(Harriet van Horne)

'Wild' Ducks

Domestication has changed the behavior of the duck. Wild ducks stick with one partner for a life-time, but domesticated males seem to have picked up bad habits from humans: they lead a polygamous life with a dozen or so females at a time.

Chapter 3

Sweet Sensations

Surprise your Honey with these deee–licious
Dream Desserts...

Sugar and spice, and all things nice—that's what love is made of...

Contents

Berry Wonderful Crush

Every spoonful of this luscious dessert will bring you a little closer to your lover's heart.

Serves 2

What to buy

- 75 g/3 oz frozen raspberries
- 175 g/6 oz Greek-style yogurt
- 2 meringues, roughly crumbled
- 1 tbsp lemon curd
- Zest of ½ lemon
- Fresh raspberries, optional

How to cook it...

Place the raspberries and yogurt in a blender, and whizz for a few seconds to form an instant soft-set ice cream.

Serve the ice cream immediately with the crumbled meringue, a little lemon curd, the grated lemon zest, and the fresh raspberries, if available. Now you'll both be having a crush!

Elephantine Sin

For some countries, it is the orange rather than the apple which is responsible for the arrival of sin in the world. Malay tradition links oranges with sin and gluttony—after overindulging, an elephant suffered from 'naga ranga', meaning fatal indigestion for elephants.

Moroccan Magic

FRESH DATES CAN BE EATEN RAW, OR USED IN SALADS OR DESSERTS SUCH AS THIS ONE. THEY ARE ESPECIALLY ABUNDANT IN WINTER AND HAVE BECOME LINKED WITH CHRISTMAS FESTIVITIES. DATES ARE DELICIOUSLY SWEET, WITH A FLAVOR AKIN TO HONEY.

Sweet Sensations

A Date and An Orange

This Moroccan classic will have you dreaming of sultry nights under gently swaying palms.

Serves 2

What to buy

- 2 large oranges
- Juice of 1 orange
- 3 tbsp sweet dessert wine
- 3 fresh dates
- A handful of pine kernels

How to cook it...

⭐ Peel the two large oranges, removing all the white pith. Halve the oranges crossways and remove any seeds. Divide into half segments and arrange on two dessert plates. Combine the juice of the third orange with the wine and pour over the oranges.

⭐ Halve the dates and remove the stones. Cut the flesh into very thin strips.

⭐ Dry-roast the pine kernels until the aroma is released, then sprinkle over the oranges together with the dates.

⭐ Serve immediately, and this will be a date you'll both remember!

Mom's American Pie

Apple pie just like Mom used to make. Your sweetie will feel like a million dollars after a slice of what made America great!

Serves 6

What to buy

- 500 g/9 oz frozen short-crust pastry, defrosted
- Grated zest of 1 lemon
- 100 g/4 oz soft light brown sugar
- 2 tbsp plain (all-purpose) flour
- ½ tsp mixed spice
- 700 g/1 ½ lb cooking apples, peeled, cored and sliced
- 50 g/2 oz sultanas
- 25 g/1 oz butter
- Caster (superfine) sugar for sprinkling

How to cook it...

🍴 Heat the oven to 190°C/375°F/Gas Mark 5. Roll out two-thirds of the pastry on a floured work surface. Line a 20 cm/8 in deep pie dish with the pastry. Chill for 1 hour.

🍴 Mix together the zest, sugar, flour, and spice, and sprinkle a little of the mixture onto the pastry in the dish.

🍴 Cover the pastry base with half the apples, sprinkle with half the sultanas, and half the remaining sugar mixture. Repeat with the remaining ingredients and dot with butter. Brush the pastry edge with a little milk or water.

⭐ Roll out the remaining pastry and use to cover the pie. Seal the edges and trim any excess. Cut a slit in the top, brush with milk, and sprinkle with caster (superfine) sugar. Bake for about 30-40 minutes, or until golden brown. Serve with a delicious cup of hot chocolate.

Apple pie without cheese is like a kiss without a squeeze...
(Folk Saying)

As American As Pie

The expression "as American as apple pie" is surprisingly new: it only became common currency in the 1960s.

Angelic Amaretto Soufflé

Sweet as a lover's kiss, this heavenly dessert is a divine
treat for your very own angel.

Serves 4-6

What to buy

- 100 g/4 oz caster (superfine) sugar
- 6 amaretto biscuits (cookies), coarsely crushed
- 90 ml/3 fl oz amaretto liqueur
- 4 eggs, separated, plus I egg white
- A pinch of salt
- 2 tbsp plain (all-purpose) flour
- 250 ml/9 fl oz milk
- A pinch of salt
- Icing (confectioner's) sugar, for dusting

How to cook it...

⭐ Heat the oven to 200°C/400°F/Gas
Mark 6. Thoroughly butter a 1.5 liter/2 ½ pint
soufflé dish and sprinkle it with a little of the
caster (superfine) sugar.

⭐ Put the crushed biscuits (cookies) in a
separate bowl. Sprinkle with 2 tbsp liqueur and
set aside. In another bowl, mix the egg yolks, flour,
and 2 tbsp of the sugar.

⭐ Heat the milk in a heavy pan. When it is
almost boiling, stir it into the egg mixture. Pour the
mixture back into the pan, set over a low heat and
simmer gently for 3-4 minutes or until thickened.
Remove from the heat and gradually add the
remaining liqueur, stirring all the time.

In a clean bowl, whisk the 5 egg whites until they hold soft peaks. Add the salt and the remaining sugar and continue whisking until stiff.

Gently fold the whites into the liqueur mixture, a bit at a time. Spoon half the mixture into the soufflé dish. Cover with a layer of the moistened biscuits (cookies), then spoon the remaining soufflé mixture on top.

Bake for 20 minutes or until the soufflé is risen and lightly browned. Sprinkle with sifted icing sugar and serve immediately, with a loving sigh.

Sugared almonds are like love taken in the form of pills... (Anon)

Breath of Love

The word "soufflé" comes from the French "souffler" which means breathing. Airy and light, like a lover's sweet sigh, this soufflé is but a mere breeze on your tongue.

Ice cream is exquisite. What a pity it isn't illegal... (Voltaire)

Love me Tender

The great Elvis Presley, crooner of some of the smoochiest love songs ever, was very fond of all sorts of sweets. His final meal consisted of four scoops of ice cream and six chocolate chip cookies.

Heaven Scent?

THE SCENT OF VANILLA IS SO INTOXICATING THAT AN AFFLICTION HAS BEEN NAMED AFTER IT: VANILLISM. WORKERS WHO HANDLE LARGE QUANTITIES EVERY DAY, MAY BECOME DRUGGED, AND SUFFER HEADACHES, WEARINESS, AND RASHES. JUST WATCH YOUR BABE FOR ADVERSE REACTIONS!

Ice Cream Attractions

Spoil your sweetie with this voluptuous ice cream confection. You'll get your just desserts!

Serves 4

What to buy

- 🍬 8 chocolate chip and nut cookies
- 🍬 2 tbsp sherry
- 🍬 2 thick slices vanilla ice cream, cut from a block
- 🍬 75 ml/3 fl oz whipped cream
- 🍬 Crumbled chocolate flake

How to cook it...

⭐ Using a small, very sharp knife, trim a bit off one edge of each cookie. Dip each cookie in sherry to moisten, making sure it won't get too soggy.

⭐ Place the ice cream slices on a cold serving platter. Press 2 cookies, trimmed side at the bottom, with their flat sides against the ice cream slices.

⭐ Carefully press the ice cream block together. Spread the cream over top and sides and decorate.

⭐ Cut the block into quarters so that each piece contains a slice of ice cream sandwiched between two cookies. Serve straight away, and feel yourselves drawn toward each other as if by a powerful magnet.

Sweet Sensations

"Tiramisu"

This sensuous dessert from the home of romance will have you and your baby serenading each other.

Serves 2

What to buy

- 🥄 **I egg, separated**
- 🥄 I tbsp caster (superfine) sugar
- 🥄 75 g/3 oz mascarpone
- 🥄 3 tbsp strong espresso coffee
- 🥄 I tbsp rum
- 🥄 40 g/I ½ oz sponge fingers
- 🥄 I5 g/I oz plain chocolate, chopped
- 🥄 I tsp cocoa powder

How to cook it...

⭐ Put the egg yolk in a bowl with the sugar and whisk to a light, pale mousse.

⭐ In a separate large bowl, stir the mascarpone to soften, then gradually beat in the egg yolk and sugar mixture.

⭐ In a third bowl beat the egg white until it forms soft peaks. Gently fold into the mascarpone mixture and put to one side.

⭐ Cut the sponge fingers in half, then pour over the coffee and rum.

⭐ In two 200ml/7fl oz glasses, put first a layer of sponge fingers, then spread with the mascarpone mixture and top with the chocolate. Repeat the layers, finishing with a layer of chopped chocolate and a dusting of cocoa powder.

✦ Chill for several hours, then serve with more espresso if you can stand the pace, or with a shot of rum, to calm you down.

Researchers have discovered that chocolate produces some of the same reactions in the brain as marijuana. (They) also discovered other similarities between the two but can't remember what they are...
(Matt Lauer)

All-Night Lovin'

"Tira–mi–su" literally means "pull me over" in Italian, and accordingly it is the romantics' dessert there. Courting couples are known to order it as a come-on. It's the perfect dessert after pasta, too, giving you an instant energy boost for more canoodling fun.

Fluffy Cloud Cakes

"That one looks like a lion." Let your imagination—and fingers—wander as you linger over these delicious soufflé desserts.

Serves 2

What to buy

- 4 tbsp sugar
- 1 tbsp cornflour (cornstarch)
- A pinch of salt
- 125 ml/4 fl oz/½ cup milk
- 50 g/2 oz dark chocolate, finely chopped
- 1 tbsp unsalted butter
- 1 large egg, separated, plus 1 large egg white
- ½ tsp grated orange zest
- 1 tbsp orange liqueur
- ½ tsp vanilla extract
- Icing (confectioner's) sugar, for dusting
- 1 large orange, peeled, segmented and chilled

How to cook it...

① Heat the oven to 200°C/400°F/Gas Mark 6. Butter two 300 ml/10 fl oz molds and sprinkle with 1 tbsp sugar, tapping out the excess. Place on a baking sheet.

② In a small saucepan, combine the cornflour (cornstarch), remaining sugar and salt, and gradually whisk in the milk over a low heat to a smooth paste. Remove from the heat. Add chocolate and butter. Let stand for 3 minutes, then whisk until smooth and melted. Whisk in the egg yolk, orange zest, liqueur, and vanilla.

③ In a bowl, beat the egg whites until stiff but not dry. Stir about a quarter of the whites into the chocolate mixture. Transfer to the bowl with the

remaining egg whites. Gently fold in until combined.
Transfer to the prepared molds.

 Bake for about 20 minutes, or until the
soufflé is risen. Remove from oven and let stand
for 5 minutes.

Run a knife around insides of the molds to
release. Tip the molds onto dessert plates and free
the contents. Dust with sugar. Arrange orange
segments on top of each cake, and whisper sweet
nothings into your darling's ears.

Love and eggs are best when they are fresh... (Russian Proverb)

Mobile Eggs

According to the Guinness
Book of Records, the record for
throwing a fresh egg without
breaking it is 317 feet, 10 inches.
There is a more romantic way,
though: in the film Tampopo, a
gangster and his moll passed a
raw egg yolk from mouth to
mouth, until—eventually—it broke!

Wine is sunlight, held together by water...
(Galileo Galilei)

Pep-up with Pepper

Pepper is rarely used in sweets, although it enhances the flavor of fruits such as strawberries. Some Indian sources recommend drinking a glass of milk with six crushed peppercorns and four crushed almonds a day. It is meant to act as a nerve tonic and as an aphrodisiac!

Passion or not?

THE PASSION FRUIT, SADLY, IS NOT NAMED FOR THE STRONG EMOTIONS IT ROUSES. INSTEAD, IT IS THOUGHT TO RESEMBLE THE CROWN OF THORNS WORN DURING THE PASSION AND CRUCIFIXION OF CHRIST. BUT THEN, WHO KNOWS WHAT THE EFFECT IS GOING TO BE? JUST TRY IT OUT.

Hot-and-Cold Love Cups

Spice up your life with a dollop of hot passion—and you'll both soon go weak at the knees...

What to buy

- 2 portions of your favorite ice cream
- 5 passion fruits
- 2 tbsp white wine
- 2 tbsp orange juice
- 1 tbsp sugar
- 1 tbsp butter
- Freshly ground black pepper

How to cook it...

⭐ Halve the passion fruits and scrape out the flesh with a teaspoon.

⭐ Place the passion fruit flesh into a small saucepan, together with the wine, orange juice, and sugar and bring to the boil. Reduce the heat and simmer gently for 10 minutes.

⭐ Sieve the sauce to remove the seeds. Cut the butter in small pieces and stir in. Season with a little black pepper.

⭐ Serve the hot sauce poured over the cold ice cream—and watch your honeypie go hot and cold.

Orange trees, trees that I love, your flowers have scented all the air I breathe...
(La Fontaine)

A Year of Puddings

Citrus fruit are available all year round, but typical summer puddings are made with fresh summer fruit such as redcurrants and raspberries. If you're seeing your sweetheart later in the year, use blackberries, plums, apples, or pears instead.

Staying Alive

CITRUS FRUIT ARE HIGH IN VITAMIN C CONTENT, A VITAL PART OF YOUR DAILY INTAKE. VITAMIN C ACTS AS AN ANTIOXIDANT, PROTECTING US FROM CANCER AND HEART DISEASE. IT IS ALSO A GENERAL IMMUNE BOOSTER. SO IF YOU WANT TO CARRY ON LOVING EACH OTHER, MAKE SURE YOU EAT PLENTY OF ORANGES AND LEMONS!

Sweet Sensations

Zesty Citrus Pudding

Treat your lover to this super summer pudding—it's full of zest, just like you'll be after eating it!

Serves 2

What to buy

- **3 slices of crusty bread**
- 25 g/l oz butter
- 40 g/l ½ oz sultanas
- 25 g/l oz soft light brown sugar
- 300 ml/10 fl oz milk
- l egg
- Grated zest of ½ orange and ½ lemon

How to cook it...

⭐ Butter the bread, quarter the slices, and arrange half in a greased ovenproof dish. Sprinkle over most of the sultanas and half the sugar.

⭐ Top with the remaining bread pieces, butter-side up, and sprinkle over the remaining sugar.

⭐ Beat milk, egg, and most of the zest together, and pour over the bread. Leave to stand for 1 hour.

⭐ Heat the oven to 150°C/300°F/Gas Mark 2. Bake the pudding for 50–60 minutes, until set and sunshine colored.

⭐ Sprinkle with the reserved sultanas and grated zest, then share the pudding with your favorite person and drift away into romantic moods.

Life is uncertain: eat dessert first... (Anon)

Really Hot Chocolate

Montezuma, the Aztec ruler, drank 50 golden goblets of hot chocolate every day. It was not the hot chocolate we know today: instead it was thick, dyed red and flavored with chili peppers. You could try this on your sweetheart—unless you're worried about Montezuma's revenge!

Tropical Fruit Fondue

Set sail for paradise with this sunshine-island delight—close your eyes and you can almost hear the parakeets!

Serves 2

What to buy

- 50 g/2 oz butter
- 1 mango, peeled and cut into chunks
- 3 pineapple rings, cut into chunks
- 25 g/1 oz caster (superfine) sugar
- 200 g/7 oz dark chocolate, broken into chunks
- 150 ml/5 fl oz double (heavy) cream

How to cook it...

⭐ Melt half the butter in a frying pan, add the mango and pineapple and fry for 1-2 minutes. Sprinkle over the sugar and continue cooking over a low heat for about 5-10 minutes, until the fruit is caramelized and golden brown.

⭐ Make the sauce: put chocolate and the remaining butter in a bowl set over a pan with boiling water. Stir until completely melted, then add the cream. Stir to mix and pour into a bowl.

⭐ To enjoy this finger-lickin' favorite, skewer a fruit chunk onto a wooden skewer, dip it in the chocolate sauce and then place between your honey's sweet, lovin' lips.

Chapter 4

Sealed with a Kiss

Show your Sweetheart you Care
with these Edible Gifts...

The gift of
love is the
sweetest thing...

Contents

Romantic Rum Truffles

Give your honey a taste of the Caribbean with these exoctic confections of chocolate, coconut, and rum.

Makes 20

What to buy

- 125 g/4 ½ oz dark chocolate
- A small knob of butter
- 2 tbsp rum
- 50 g/2 oz desiccated coconut
- 100 g/4 oz cake crumbs
- 75 g/3 oz icing (confectioner's) sugar
- 2 tbsp cocoa powder

How to cook it...

⭐ Break the chocolate into pieces and melt with the butter in a bowl set over a pan of boiling water.

⭐ Remove from the heat and beat in the rum. Stir in the desiccated coconut, cake crumbs and 50 g/2 oz of the icing sugar. Beat until combined.

⭐ Roll the mixture into small balls, place them on a sheet of baking paper and chill until firm.

⭐ Sift the remaining icing sugar on one plate and the cocoa powder on another. Roll half the truffles in icing sugar and the remainder in the cocoa powder. Place the truffles in paper cases to present them to your sweetheart.

Sealed with a Kiss

Funny Valentine's Cake

Serve this exotic gateau to your sweetie on Valentine's Day and romance is sure to be on the cards!

Makes 1 cake

What to buy

- 100 g/4 oz butter
- 150 g/5 oz sugar
- 2 large eggs
- 300 g/12 oz plain (all-purpose) flour
- 5 tsp baking powder
- 100 g/4 oz toasted wheat germ
- 150 ml/5 fl oz /1²/3 cups milk
- 1 tsp vanilla extract
- ½ tsp almond extract
- Grated zest of half a lemon
- 450 g/1 lb mixed dried fruit, chopped
- Icing (confectioner's) sugar for dusting

How to cook it...

⭐ Heat the oven to 180°C/350°F/Gas Mark 4. In a bowl, cream together the butter and the sugar until fluffy. Beat in the eggs, until mixed well.

⭐ In a second bowl, combine the flour, baking powder, and wheat germ, then in a third bowl, combine the milk with the vanilla extract, almond extract, and lemon zest. Add both the dry and the liquid ingredients to the creamed butter and mix together until well combined. Gently fold in the mixed dried fruits.

⭐ Pour the batter into a well-greased and floured 2 liter/4 pint/2 quart baking tin. Bake for about 1 hour, or until a knife inserted in center of the cake comes out clean. Let the cake cool in the oven for about 10 minutes, then turn it out and leave to cool completely on a wire rack.

 Brew a pot of aromatic coffee and cuddle up to your sweet Valentine for an afternoon treat. Play your favorite records and dream of romantic times to come.

Love is a snowmobile racing across the tundra and then suddenly it flips over, pinning you underneath...
(Matt Groening)

The first Valentine

The origins of Valentine's Day are uncertain. There may have been a real Valentine, a 3rd-century priest who defied the Emperor Claudius II's ban on war-time marriages and secretly married couples, until he was discovered and put to death.

Sugar and Spice Heart

Who could resist a sweet treat with a hint of spice? Melt your honey's heart with this taste-full token of your affections.

Makes 1 large heart

What to buy

- 200 g/7 oz self-raising flour
- 1 tsp cinnamon
- 2 tsp ground ginger
- 50 g/2 oz butter
- 50 g/2 oz dark brown sugar
- 2 tbsp black molasses
- 1 tbsp golden (corn) syrup
- Grated zest of 1 orange
- 1 tbsp icing (confectioner's) sugar
- Red food coloring

How to cook it...

① Heat the oven to 180°C/350°F/Gas Mark 4. Sift the flour, cinnamon, and ginger into a mixing bowl.

② In a saucepan, melt the butter, sugar, molasses, and syrup over a low heat. Remove from the heat, stir in the zest, and pour the mixture into the flour. Mix to form a soft dough. Leave to rest for at least 30 minutes.

③ Roll out the dough to 5 mm/⅛ in thick and with a knife cut a large heart, reshaping as necessary. Bake the heart on a greased baking sheet for about 10-15 minutes until just set and beginning to brown. Remove and let cool.

✪ Mix the icing sugar with a few drops of water to form a thick paste. Blend in the food coloring, stir until all is well blended and leaves a trail. Spoon into a paper piping bag, snip off the corner and pipe your lover's name and your personal message on top of the heart. Leave to set.

✪ Pack the heart in a pink box, decorate with pink ribbons, and expedite it to your loved one.

Love is an irresistible desire to be irresistibly desired...
(Robert Frost)

Love and Spice

In Germany and Austria, the gingerbread heart with a piped love message is a traditional love token, perhaps because ginger, one of the main ingredients, has been reputed to have aphrodisiac powers since Roman times!

Magic Chocolate Peaches

See your lover's eyes light up when you present these 'charming' fruit—truly a taste of paradise!

Makes 20 fruits

What to buy

- 100 g/4 oz dried peaches, finely chopped
- 3 tbsp brandy
- 15 g/½ oz desiccated coconut
- 90 g/3 ½ oz dark chocolate
- 30 g/2 oz white chocolate

How to cook it...

⭐ In a bowl, soak the chopped peaches in the brandy for about 1 hour, or until the brandy has been completely absorbed.

⭐ Dry-fry the coconut in a hot frying pan, stirring all the time, until it is evenly golden. Break up the dark chocolate and melt in a bowl set over a pan with boiling water.

⭐ Add the melted chocolate and the coconut to the peach and brandy mixture and stir to combine all the ingredients.

⭐ Shape the mixture into teaspoon-sized ovals. Grease a baking sheet and place the peach shapes on the sheet.

Melt the white chocolate in a bowl set over a saucepan of simmering water, place it in a piping bag and decorate the brandy peaches with white chocolate swirls and patterns. Leave to set.

Place the chocolate peaches in a box, cover with velvet, silk, or lacy ribbons, and have it delivered to the special person in your life.

Forget love, I'd rather fall in chocolate... (Anon)

Heavenly Nut

All parts of the coconut and the tree on which it grows are used by humans. The nut itself, although deliciously rich, contains no cholesterol and is easy to digest. So just take your honey on that sunny Caribbean cruise!

Sealed with a Kiss

Melt-in-the-Mouth Cherries

Candy doesn't come any sweeter than this! Sheer bliss in every mouthful.

Makes 30

What to buy

- 30 maraschino cherries, with stems
- 1 ½ tbsp butter, softened
- 1 ½ tbsp light golden (corn) syrup
- A pinch of salt
- 225 g/8 oz caster (superfine) sugar
- 350 g/12 oz dark chocolate

How to cook it...

⭐ Drain the cherries, and place them on kitchen paper to dry. In a bowl, combine the butter, golden (corn) syrup, sugar, and salt. Knead the mixture until it becomes very smooth. Cover with clingfilm (plastic wrap) and chill for about 10 minutes to set.

⭐ Take a cherry in your hand and 1 teaspoon of the sugar mixture. Carefully shape the mixture around each cherry. Place the covered cherries on a greased baking sheet, cover and chill for about 30 minutes to set the coating.

⭐ Melt the chocolate in a bowl set over a pan of simmering water. Holding the cherries by their stems, dip them into the melted chocolate, one at a time. Add extra chocolate with a spoon to make sure the cherries are evenly coated all over. Chill again, until the chocolate is hardened.

 Keep the cherries in a cool place in a covered box until the time is right—perhaps you are ready to propose?—then present them to your darling on your very special day.

Life is a bowl of cherries... (Popular Saying)

Darkly Delicious

There are many types of chocolate —as any chocoholic will know! For cooking, dark chocolate is the most commonly used. Its cocoa content is between 30% and 75%, and a higher content will give a richer, more intense flavor. Spoil your darling—go for the best you can get.

Sealed with a Kiss

Mexican Hearts

Give these hearts to the one you love. One taste and your honey's heart will be yours forever.

Makes about 8

What to buy

🍬 A pinch of salt
🍬 A strand of saffron
🍬 150 g/5 oz flour
🍬 Oil for deep-frying
🍬 Icing (confectioner's) sugar
🍬 Ground cinnamon

How to cook it...

⭐ Put the salt and the saffron into a saucepan, add 225 ml/8 fl oz/1 cup water, and bring to the boil, stirring constantly. Take the pan off the heat and tip in all the flour in one go. Knead with a hand-held whisk until a thick batter is formed which easily comes off the edges of the pan. Leave to cool for about 10 minutes.

⭐ Meanwhile, heat the oil in a deep-fryer to 180°C/350°F. Cut a few sheets of baking paper to the same diameter as the deep-fryer, grease the sheets, then chill them in the fridge.

⭐ Fill the batter into a piping bag with a star nozzle. Take the greased paper out of the fridge and pipe heart-shapes on it. Lift up the paper with the hearts, turn it over and drop the sheet and the hearts together into the hot oil. Now, using tongs, carefully pull off the paper. Close the lid and deep-fry the hearts

for 3 minutes, turn them over and fry the other side. Lift out the hearts with a slotted spoon, drain on kitchen paper. Dust with icing sugar and cinnamon, and send to your sweet post-haste.

Homer: See, Marge, I TOLD you they could deep-fry my shirt. Marge: I didn't say they couldn't, I said they shouldn't... (The Simpsons)

Hasta la vista, baby

These Mexican hearts are based on the recipe for Churros, the famous deep-fried Mexican snack that has become popular around the world. To enjoy them at their best, dunk the hearts in delicious hot chocolate and share them with your baby.

Pink Delites

Sweets for your sweet—these delectable cookies will assure your place in your baby's affections.

Makes about 60

What to buy

- 200 g/7 oz flour
- 500 g/1lb 2 oz icing (confectioner's) sugar
- 200 g/7 oz ground almonds
- 200 g/7 oz butter, cut into dice
- 1 egg
- A pinch of salt
- ½ vanilla pod
- Grated zest of 1 lemon
- A pinch of cinnamon
- 200 g/7 oz raspberry jelly
- About 4 tbsp lemon juice
- 2 tbsp raspberry-flavored schnapps

How to cook it...

Heat the oven to 150°C/300°F/Gas Mark 2. Put the flour into a bowl, and make a hollow in the center. Add 150 g/3 oz of the icing (confectioner's) sugar, almonds, butter, egg, salt, vanilla, zest and cinnamon. Knead to a smooth dough, wrap in a towel, and chill for 1 hour.

Roll out the dough, about 6 mm/1/4 in thick and cut out ovals, circles, hearts or other shapes. Place on a baking tray lined with baking paper and bake for 15 minutes, or until light brown. Take out and leave to cool.

Heat the raspberry jelly in a saucepan and reduce a little. In a bowl, combine the remaining icing (confectioner's) sugar with the lemon juice

and schnapps to make a glaze. Brush the cookies
with the liquid jelly and leave to set a little, then
coat them with the schnapps glaze and leave to
harden completely.

 Pack in a pretty box and present your gift to
your sweet baby, together with a single pink rose.

Don't eat too many
almonds; they add
weight to the breasts...
(Colette)

Sweet Sugar

In the 19th century, sugar was
the elixir of pleasure for the rich—
Goethe paid 2.7 gold marks for
one kilogram! Today sugar is
still covetable and, like all things
sweet, it has been closely
associated with love—as in
sweetheart, honey, and sugar!

Sealed with a Kiss

Cupid's Cookies

**Give Cupid a helping hand with these candied cookies—
each one will fly like an arrow straight to your baby's heart!**

Makes about 15

What to buy

- 🍬 150 g/5 oz raw marzipan, chopped
- 🍬 75 g/3 oz icing (confectioner's) sugar
- 🍬 1 egg white
- 🍬 15 g/½ oz dried orange zest, finely chopped
- 🍬 100 g/4 oz almond flakes
- 🍬 100 g/4 oz orange marmalade
- 🍬 100 g/4 oz dark chocolate

How to cook it...

⭐ Heat the oven to 190°C/375°F/Gas Mark 5. Put the marzipan into a bowl, sift the icing (confectioner's) sugar into the bowl, add the egg white. Knead until you have a light, smooth mixture. Mix in the orange zest.

⭐ With a teaspoon, remove small portions and place on a baking tray lined with baking paper. Cover densely with almond flakes, then bake for about 8–10 minutes.

⭐ Spread half the cookies with the marmalade, then sandwich them together. Heat the chocolate in a bowl set over a pan with boiling water, dip one side of each cookie in the chocolate, then place on a rack to cool and dry.

Play Cupid: get a box of these delicious cookies and deliver it to your true love in person, perhaps with a bottle of Amaretto or another sweet dessert wine to sip together.

Broken cookies don't have calories... (Anon)

Never Go Hungry

Marzipan was originally invented to cope with a drought that left plentiful almonds but no wheat. Today, couples are often given marzipan before they are wed, so they will never go hungry.

All alcoholic drinks, rightly use
are good for body and soul afil
but as a restorative of both the
is nothing like brandy...
(George Sainsbury)

Flames of Desire

Alcohol is known to heighten desire, mainly because it removes inhibitions. Share these fruits with your own sugar plum and check if it's true. Serve a glass of the same brandy you used for the plums as a drink. Briefly soak a sugar cube in the brandy, place it on a teaspoon, and balance the spoon on the rim of your glass. Set light to it, and watch the flames of passion consume you both—and the melted sugar drizzle into your drink!

Brandy Galore

ONE OF THE BEST BRANDIES TO USE FOR THESE PLUMS IS ARMAGNAC, A TYPE OF BRANDY MADE FROM PLUMS IN THE SOUTH-WEST OF FRANCE. YOU COULD ALSO TRY OTHER PERFECT COMBINATIONS OF FRUIT AND ALCOHOL, SUCH AS CHERRIES IN KIRSCH, PINEAPPLE IN RUM, OR APPLES IN CALVADOS.

Sealed with a Kiss

Passionate Plums

These fervent fruit will light a fire in your lover's heart—just like them, you'll be consumed with passion.

Makes 1 large jar

What to buy

- 250 g/9 oz perfect plums
- 175 g/6 oz sugar
- 1 clove
- 1 short piece of cinnamon stick
- Brandy

How to cook it...

⚝ Place the plums into a saucepan of 90 ml/ 3 fl oz water together with the sugar, clove, and cinnamon. Bring to the boil, then take off the heat and stand in a cool place for 2 days.

⚝ Lift out the plums with a slotted spoon. Return the saucepan to the heat and cook until the juices are reduced to a syrup. Remove and leave to cool, then top up with an equal quantity of brandy.

⚝ Sterilize a jar in boiling water, then place the plums in the jar. Pour over the brandy-syrup and close the jar firmly with preserving foil.

⚝ Label the jar with your special love message.

Sealed with a Kiss

Heavenly Strawberry Cheesecake

**Prove you're an angel by serving up this celestial confection
—your baby will be singing your praises to the rooftops!**

Makes 1 cake

What to buy

- 50 g/2 oz butter
- 75 g/3 oz plain (all-purpose) flour
- 75 g/3 oz caster (superfine) sugar
- 700 g/1 ½ lb cottage cheese
- 2 eggs
- Grated zest of 1 lemon
- 4 tbsp natural yogurt
- 225 g/8 oz fresh strawberries

How to cook it...

① Heat the oven to 180°C/350°F/Gas Mark 4. Meanwhile, grease and line a 20 cm/8 in loose-bottomed cake tin.

② Melt the butter in a saucepan, them combine with the flour and one-third of the sugar until well mixed. Put into the base of the cake tin and bake for 10 minutes.

③ Meanwhile, put the cottage cheese into a bowl. Beat the eggs into the cheese. Add the lemon zest, the yogurt, and the remaining sugar and beat well together to combine.

④ Fill the mixture into the cake tin, and bake for a further 20 minutes. Remove the tin and leave to cool for several hours.

✪ Carefully remove the cake from the tin. Slice the strawberries and arrange them in a heart shape on top of the cake. Deliver the cake to your darling in person, with vanilla-flavored whipped cream, a bunch of roses, and a winning smile. Take along a video of your favorite slushy movie to watch together, while you're holding hands.

Doubtless God could have made a better berry, but doubtless God never did... (William Butler)

Memorable Berries

Not only are they delicious, strawberries are also very good for you. Apart from numerous other benefits, the spring-harbinger berries have been found to protect against stress in the brain, which improves your memory—so you'll never forget a birthday or anniversary again!

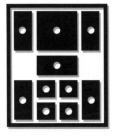